JACK
THE
TREACLE EATER

Charles Causley is one of our most distinguished living poets. Apart from six years in the wartime Royal Navy he has lived almost all his life in his native town of Launceston, Cornwall, where he also once worked as a teacher. He has published many collections of his work both for adults and for children, and has been the recipient of a number of literary awards and prizes, including the Kurt Maschler Award and the Signal Poetry Award and (from the USA) the Ingersoll/T. S. Eliot Award. He is a Companion of Literature, an honour awarded by the Royal Society of Literature, and has received the Queen's Gold Medal for poetry. In 1986 he was appointed CBE.

Tony Ross was a teacher, graphic designer and cartoonist before becoming a well-known illustrator and author of children's books. He has written and illustrated nearly seventy titles and has illustrated a further 450. He has won awards in Germany, Holland and the US, and there have been exhibitions of his work in Europe and Japan. He enjoys sailing and travelling in his spare time, and he lives with his wife and daughter in Cheshire.

'An impressive collection' *Observer*

'Causley at his best – witty and lyrical, lovely rounded poems which leap from the page and demand to be read out loud . . . a boxful of jewels'
Western Morning News

'Will set [children] on the road to loving poetry for life'
Mother

───────────

By the same author

Figgie Hobbin

The Young Man of Cury

All Day Saturday

Early in the Morning

Going to the Fair

Collected Poems for Children

Selected Poems for Children

JACK
THE
TREACLE EATER
and other poems

Charles Causley

Illustrated by Tony Ross

MACMILLAN CHILDREN'S BOOKS

To Cynthia and Stanley Simmonds

First published 1987 by Macmillan Children's Books
This edition published 2002 by Macmillan Children's Books
a division of Macmillan Publishers Limited
20 New Wharf Road, London N1 9RR
Basingstoke and Oxford
www.panmacmillan.com

Associated companies throughout the world

ISBN 0 330 39978 0

Text copyright © Charles Causley 1987
Illustrations copyright © Tony Ross 2002

The right of Charles Causley and Tony Ross to be identified as the
author and illustrator of this book has been asserted by them in accordance
with the Copyright, Designs and Patents Act 1988.

1 3 5 7 9 8 6 4 2

A CIP catalogue record for this book is available from the British Library.

Printed by Mackays of Chatham plc, Chatham, Kent.

Contents

MORNING
NOON AND NIGHT

Count Pollen

Count Pollen walked his English land
Under the summer blue.
'County, good day to you!' I cried.
   Tchoo! said the Count. *A-tchoo!*

The noon was bright, a thirsty sun
Had swallowed up the dew.
'I trust I find you well?' I asked.
   Tchoo! said the Count. *A-tchoo!*

The softest breezes from the south
Among the grasses blew.
'How sweet,' I called, 'the summer air!'
   Tchoo! said the Count. *A-tchoo!*

Along the valley floor the stream
Its silver waters drew.
'Is good to be alive!' I cried.
   Tchoo! said the Count. *A-tchoo!*

'In all of England,' I remarked,
'Was never such a view –
Ah, do you not agree, my Lord?'
　　Tchoo! said the Count. *A-tchoo!*

'There's never a one who does not wish
He was,' I said, 'as you.
But why the tears upon your cheek?'
　　Tchoo! said the Count. *A-tchoo!*

When I Was a Hundred and Twenty-six

When I was a hundred and twenty-six
And you were a hundred and four
What fun, my dearest dear, we had
At the back of the Co-op store.
It was all such a very long time ago
That it seems just like a dream
In the days when you called me your own
   Rich Tea
And you were my Custard Cream.

Such joys we knew with those dinners
  à deux
At the bottom of the parking lot
On roasted gnu and buffalo stew
And Tandoori chicken in a pot.
Such songs, my love, we used to sing
Till the stars had lost their shine,
And the bells of heaven rang
   ding, ding, ding
And the neighbours rang 999.

When I was a hundred and twenty-six
And you were a hundred and four
We thought love's cherry would last a very
Long time, and then some more.
But days are fleet when ways are sweet
As the honey in a hive –
And I am a hundred and twenty-seven
And you are a hundred and five.

I've Never Seen the Milkman

I've never seen the milkman,
His shiny cap or coat.
I've never seen him driving
His all-electric float.

When he comes by the morning's
As black as printers' ink.
I've never heard his footstep
Nor a single bottle clink.

No matter if it's foggy
Or snow is on the ground,
Or rain or hail or half a gale
He always does his round.

I wonder if he's thin or fat
Or fair or dark or bald,
Or short or tall, and most of all
I wonder what he's called.

He goes to bed so early
That not an owl has stirred,
And rises up again before
The earliest early bird.

God bless the faithful milkman,
My hero – and that's flat!
Or perhaps he's a milklady?
(I never thought of that.)

Jackie Grimble

Here's Jackie Grimble
Looking in the window
Pointing at the mountain
Pointing at the moor.
Shall we walk together
In the golden weather?
Calls Jackie Grimble.
That's what it's for!

Here's Jackie Grimble
With his arms akimbo
Winks a wicked eye at me
As if to say,
Never mind your master,
The clock is beating faster,
The sun will be a cinder
Before the end of day.

Here's Jackie Grimble
Thinner than a spindle
Pointing where the emerald
Grasses grow.
Why must you labour
With pencil and with paper,
Says Jackie Grimble,
When the sun shines so?

Ah, but Jackie Grimble
The air is growing nimble,
A white wind is rising
That smells of snow.
Under the green riding
The tall mire is hiding
And the sands are quick
Wherever I go.

Here's Jackie Grimble
No bigger than a thimble
Dancing, advancing
Down from the tor.
*Lie in the clover
Before the summer's over,*
Cries Jack Grimble,
That's what it's for!

Maggie Dooley

Old Maggie Dooley
Twice a day
Comes to the Park
To search for the stray,
Milk in a bowl,
Scraps on a tray,
'Breakfast time!' 'Supper time!'
Hear her say.

Alone on a bench
She'll sit and wait
Till out of the bushes
They hesitate:
Tommy No-Tail
And Sammy No-Fur,
Half-Eye Sally
And Emmy No-Purr.

She sits by the children's
Roundabout
And takes a sip
From a bottle of stout.
She smiles a smile
And nods her head
Until her little
Family's fed.

Whatever the weather,
Shine or rain,
She comes at eight
And eight again.
'It's a Saint you are,'
To Maggie I said,
But she smiled a smile
And shook her head.

'Tom and Sammy,
Sally and Em,
They need me
And I need them.
I need them
And they need me.
That's all there is,'
She said, said she.

Twenty-four Hours

Twenty-four hours
　　Make a night and a day;
Never a minute
　　More will one stay.

One o'clock sounds
　　To the owl's cold cry;
Two, as the flame of the fox
　　Glimmers by.

Three, the still hour
　　Of the moon and the star;
Four, the first cock-crow
　　Is heard from afar.

Five, and the bird-song
　　Already begun;
Six, the bright mail van
　　Comes up with the sun.

Seven, here's the milk
　　With the butter and cream;
Eight, all the kettles
　　Are letting off steam.

Nine, the school bell
 Calls the lazy and late;
Ten, as the children
 Chant, 'Two fours are eight.'

Eleven, and it's cooking
 With pot, pan and spoon;
Twelve, and the morning
 Says, 'Good afternoon!'

One, and for dinner
 Hot pudding and pie;
Two, all the dishes
 Are watered and dry.

Three, the quick water-hen
 Hides in the pool;
Four, as the children
 Come smiling from school.

Five, see the milking cows
 Lurch down the lane;
Six, and the family
 Together again.

Seven, and the children
 Are bathed and in bed;
Eight, dad is snoozing
 The paper unread.

Nine, and the house mouse
    Squints out of his hole;
Ten, and the tabby cat
    Takes a dark stroll.

Eleven, bolt the window
    And lock the front door;
Twelve o'clock strikes
    And on sea and on shore
Night and day's journey
    Is starting once more.
Twelve o'clock sounds
    On the steep and the plain,
Day and night's journey
    Beginning again.

Twenty-four hours
    Make a night and a day;
Never a minute
    More will one stay.
Never a moment
    Will one delay.
So much to do
    And so much to say:
Why must they always
    Hurry away?

Lady Jane Grey

Lady Jane Grey
  Went on her way
Out of her house
  On the first of May.

The blackbird whistled,
  The blackbird sang
And all the bells
  Of England rang.

She went to the palace.
  She sat her down.
She wore the Queen
  Of England's crown.

She wore it a week
  And a day and a day
Of her sixteen years.
  Poor Lady Jane Grey.

ONE BY ONE

Kensey

Here's a card from Tangier, Kensey.
White African air.
Writing on the back says,
'Wish you were here'.

Here's a card from Kashmir, Kensey.
Fretwork mountain, snow.
Writing on the back says,
'Get up and go'.

Here's a card from Eilat, Kensey,
Snorkels, blue glass bay.
Writing on the back says,
'Sun shines all day'.

Here's a card from Rome, Kensey.
The Spanish Steps, flowers.
Writing on the back says,
'Window marked x = ours'.

Tangier, Kashmir, Kensey,
Eilat and Rome.
What say I stir myself?
Stir the fire instead, mister,
Says my old cat Kensey.
Best stay at home.

The Elephant and the Butterfly

Said the elephant to the butterfly
As they wandered the forest through,
'I wish I could rise up into the skies
And flutter about like you!
If I was as fine as a feather
I'd ramble the wide air round.
It's a terrible bore to never get more
Than a couple of feet off the ground!'

Said the butterfly to the elephant,
'My dear, that sounds perfectly fine.
You could make yourself wings out of
    palms and things
With the aid of the creeper and vine.
If you turn your trunk like a propeller
In a bit of a following breeze
There's no reason why you won't take
    to the sky
With simply incredible ease.'

Believe it or not, but no sooner
Had the butterfly uttered these words
Than the elephant flew straight up in
    the blue
As though he was one of the birds.
High over the trees of the jungle
And high above mountain and scree
The elephant wobbled and wavered
Over land and then over the sea.

'Good gracious!' he cried, and, 'Good heavens!
I'm dizzy from toe to my crown,
And my memory's bad (and isn't it sad?)
But when things go up they come down.
My head is rolling and reeling
And my stomach has gone on the spree.
I've a notion that if I don't land in the ocean
It's curtains for certain for me!'

But the lucky old elephant landed
In the softest of sea and of sand
And he paddled ashore with a bit of a roar
And sat himself down on the land.
He lifted his voice to the hill-tops
With an elephant trumpet-y sound.
'Do you think, butterfly, I was foolish to try?'
But the creature was nowhere around.

And ever since then you will
    find him
(That is, if you're anxious to
    look)
Reclining and reading an
    encyclopaedian
Sort of a Reference Book.
He studies it morning and
    evening
(Now and then gazing up in
    the sky)
On 'How Best to Sight the
    Butterfly (White)'

And a faraway look in his eye.

Rocco

I am St Roche's dog. We stand
Together on the painted wall:
His hat tricked with a cockleshell,
Wallet and staff in pilgrim hand.
He lifts a torn robe to display
The plague-spot. I sit up and wait.
A lot of us has peeled away.
My breed is indeterminate.
    Bow! Wow!

Under a Piacenza sun
The sickness struck him like a flame.
'Dear Lord,' he cried, 'my life is done!'
And to a summer forest came.
But I, his creature, sought him high
And sought him low on his green bed
Where he had lain him down to die.
I licked his wounds and brought him bread.
   Bow! Wow!

And he was healed, and to his house
Sick by the hundred seethed and swarmed
As, by God's grace, the Saint performed
Cures that were quite miraculous.
Now my good master's home is where
Are heavenly joys, which some declare
No fish nor bird nor beast may share.
Ask: Do I find this hard to bear?
   Bow! Wow!

see Notes on p.101

When George the Fifth Was a Midshipman

When George the Fifth was a Midshipman
(Before he wore the crown)
He bought himself an African Grey
Ashore in Port Said town
   God Save the King! said Charlotte.

She was quite the prettiest parrot
The Prince had ever seen.
The dragoman said she was six months old.
The Prince was seventeen.
   Shipmates for ever! said Charlotte.

She perched on the Prince's shoulder
(So to speak) for the rest of his life.
They say he loved that parrot
Almost as much as a wife.
    What about it? said Charlotte.

In HMS *Bacchante*
Three years they sailed the blue.
She'd hawk and squawk like an old
    sea-dog
When His Highness wasn't in view.
    Where's the Captain? said Charlotte.

One day at Buckingham Palace
She heard the city bells ring
And all the people of London
Cry out, 'God Save the King!'
    Me too, said Charlotte.

She sat at the right-hand corner
Of King George's royal throne.
There wasn't a single State Paper
She didn't know for her own.
 Mum's the word! said Charlotte.

When the King was ill and ailing
And very nearly died
They shut her out of the bedroom;
Left her in the passage outside.
 Bless my buttons! said Charlotte.

But when his illness was ended
She was first at His Majesty's bed;
Danced for joy on the pillow
And over his anointed head.
 God Saved the King! said Charlotte.

*King George V (1865–1936) entered the
Royal Navy when he was twelve, and
acquired Charlotte, his pet parrot (an
African Grey), when his ship called at
Port Said. She was his great friend for
most of his life. Charlotte had a loud,
commanding voice like an old-fashioned
sea-captain. Most (but not all) of the
remarks she makes in the poems are
phrases we are told she had picked up or
had been taught to say.*

Rock Ape

I have climbed a Pillar of Hercules,
A rock swimming in the Middle Sea
And named for the Moorish conqueror
Gebal-al-Tarik.

Below me, beyond the smoking cork woods
Of San Roque, the Phoenicians sailed for tin
To the dark north, the dragon guarded
Hesperides Garden and its bright apples,
And the surly prophet Jonah was hurled ashore
By a large fish.

In all Europe is no wild tribe such as mine.
I must ask you not to address me as Monkey.
My tall house is of soft grey limestone.
In my falling garden grow
Scarlet geranium, heliotrope, daphne,
The castor-oil plant and a little
Maidenhair fern.

My day is punctuated by the bugle,
Sometimes by a weeping fog from
   the east,
Sometimes by a snow-cold
   north wind
From the Serrania de Ronda.

I have seen many sieges,
Heard many speeches
In strange clacking tongues.
All say, 'I want. I want.'

On a glass-clear day I spy
The snow-jagged peaks of the Sierra Nevada
Across the oil-smooth Bay,
In Africa.

Some declare I was brought
By the dark-voiced, fierce and holy
Fathers of the Moriscos;
Others, that I came beneath the waters
Of the strait by a secret path
Known only to my tribe.
I shall not tell you what I know
Of this.

Only that I am marooned here
Since the earth broke apart,
Since the shaking of land and sea
A million days and nights
Ago. And that there will come
   a time
When sea and land shatter again
And I shall return to the great
   Sierra,
The cool snows of Africa.

see Notes on p.102

Moor-hens

Living by Bate's Pond, they
(Each spring and summer day)
Watched among reed and frond
The moor-hens prank and play.

Watched them dip and dive,
Watched them pass, re-pass,
Sputtering over the water
As if it were made of glass.

Watched them gallop the mud
Bobbing a tail, a head;
Under an April stream
Swimming with tails outspread.

Listened at night for a cry
Striking the sky like a stone;
The *kik! kik! kik!* of farewell
As they drifted south for the sun.

Whose are the children, and who
Are the children who lived by the pond,
Summer and spring year-long
When the wild sun shone?
Thirsty the stream, and dry;
Ah, and the house is gone.

Mawgan Porth

Mawgan Porth
The Siamese cat
Lives in an elegant
London flat
Dines on salmon
Sleeps on silk
Drinks Malvern water
Instead of milk
Shops at Harrods
Fortnum & Mason
Has room after room
To run and race in
Wears winter jackets
Of Harris tweed
Strolls in the park
At the end of a lead
But in case you think
As think you might
He's a bit of a drone
Or a parasite
I can tell you quite
Without a qualm
He's a perfectly wonderful
Burglar alarm
But if anyone moves
A bolt or catch
Or touches a single
Security latch
Or worst of all
(I'm certain sure)

Tries to pick the lock
On the big front door
You'll hear him skirl
And you'll hear him squeal
As if his lungs
Were made of steel
You'll hear such a bellow
You'll hear such a blare
As stops the traffic
In Belgrave Square
And for hours and hours
He screeches and squalls
Enough to crack
The dome of St Paul's
Don't you think, I said
To Mawgan Porth
(In his chair that dates
From William IV)
You're a lucky old cat
In this world of strife
To lead such a super-
Superior life?
But nothing he said
As if nothing he knew
Just kept me clearly
Under review
And fixed me firm
With his eyes of blue
His Siamese cat-ical
Aristocratical
Eyes as he gazed me
Through and through.

SOME PEOPLE

The Old Lord of Trecrogo

Long, long ago-go
The old Lord of Trecrogo
Sat in his fougu
On a green granite boulder
Under Hawk's Tor,
Round his head a band of gold,
A red-legged crow
Standing on his shoulder
And at his feet
His Wise Men four.

'Who's that at the door?'
Said the Old Lord of Trecrogo.
'Someone's been waiting
For a month or more.
What do you think
I pay you for?
Is it friend or foe,
I want to know?
Why don't you rise up
And go, go, go?'

'Might be Mazey Jack,'
Said Siblyback,
'Come Christmassing, I fear,
Wrong time of year.'
'Might be All-Made-Of-Bone,'
Hummed Woolstone
Through his ivory comb.
'If you ask me, friend,
Best to pretend
No one's at home.'

'May be Tall Tide,'
Old Craddock cried,
'Sliding ashore
Under the front door.'
'All wrong,' said Witheybrook.
'I just had a look.
To my sorrow,
I think it's Tomorrow,
Nothing less, nothing more,
Scatting on the door.'

'*Tomorrow?* Oh! Oh!'
Said the old Lord of Trecrogo.
'Tomorrow that's knocking?
Tomorrow? That's shocking!
None can outpace him.
Who'll go and face him?
Can't someone deal him
A blow, like so? Or so?'
Said the old Lord of Trecrogo.

'Not me,' said Siblyback.
'Nor me,' said Woolstone.
'Not me,' said Old Craddock.
Said Witheybrook, 'Can't be done.'
'Can't believe what I've heard!'
The old Lord averred.
'Now I have only one true friend,
I wonder, I wonder whether—'
But, 'No go! No go! No go!'
Said the red-legged crow
And never budged a feather.
    And Tomorrow came on.

Why?

Why do you turn your head, Susanna,
And why do you swim your eye?
It's only the children on Bellman Street
Calling, *A penny for the guy!*

Why do you look away, Susanna,
As the children wheel him by?
It's only a dummy in an old top-hat
And a fancy jacket and tie.

Why do you take my hand, Susanna,
As the pointing flames jump high?
It's only a bundle of sacking and straw.
Nobody's going to die.

Why is your cheek so pale, Susanna,
As the whizzbangs flash and fly?
It's nothing but a rummage of paper and rag
Strapped to a stick you spy.

Why do you say you hear, Susanna,
The sound of a last, long sigh?
And why do you say it won't leave your head
No matter how hard you try?

Best let me take your home, Susanna.
Best on your bed to lie.
It's only a dummy in an old top-hat.
Nobody's going to die.

Mr Zukovsky

When Mr Augustus Zukovsky
First met his intended-to-be
His friends they all moaned and they grizzled
   and groaned,
'You just *can't* think of marrying she!
Why, she's clumsy, they say, as a camel
(If camels *are* clumsy, that is).
The mere thought of it, Mr Zukovsky,
Is fetching us all in a fizz!

'It looks as if what she is wearing
Was fired at her out of a gun,
And the state of her hair is her mother's despair
And like rays sticking out of the sun.
While as for you, Mr Zukovsky,
You're always so sober and neat,
And it's very well known how you brush and
   you comb
Before you set off down the street.

'She's a voice like the Seven Stones Lighthouse
When it's speaking of fogs or of gales,
And if she should whisper a secret
You can hear it from Windsor to Wales.
She's no ear whatever for music
And she can't tell a sharp from a flat.
When they're playing the National Anthem
She doesn't know what they are at.

'The money it slides through her fingers,
She can't sew, she can't clean, she can't cook,
And she spends half the day (so the
    neighbours all say)
With her nose in a *poetry* book.'
But to Mr Augustus Zukovsky
Such words were a slander and shame,
And he walked up the aisle with a
    beautiful smile
And he married his love just the same.

Now Mr and Mrs Zukovsky
For twenty-five years have been wed,
And there isn't a happier couple
In the whole of the kingdom, it's said.
They've a dog and two cats and five children,
A budgie, a buck and a doe,
And you won't find a jollier family
Though you search the world high
    and then low.

And as for those friends and companions
Who prophesied nothing but woe,
They all of them cry (without winking an eye),
'But we always *said* it would be so,
They're so awf'ly well suited, you know!
Yes, we always said it would be so,
We ALWAYS said it would be so, and so,
We *always* said it would be so.'

Family Album

I wish I liked Aunt Leonora
When she draws in her breath with a hiss
And with fingers of ice and a grip like a vice
She gives me a walloping kiss.

I wish I loved Uncle Nathaniel
(The one with the teeth and the snore).
He's really a pain when he tells me *again*
About what he did in the War.

I really don't care for Aunt Millie,
Her bangles and brooches and beads,
Or the gun that she shoots or those ex-army boots
Or the terrible dogs that she breeds.

I simply can't stand Uncle Albert.
Quite frankly, he fills me with dread
When he gives us a tune with a knife, fork
    and spoon.
(I don't think he's right in the head.)

I wish I loved Hetty and Harry
(Aunt Hilary's horrible twins)
As they lie in their cots giving
    off lots and lots
Of gurgles and gargles and grins.

As for nieces or nephews or cousins
There seems nothing else one can do
Except sit in a chair and exchange a cold stare
As if we came out of a Zoo.

Though they say blood is thicker than water,
I'm not at all certain it's so.
If you think it's the case, kindly write to this space.
It's something I'm anxious to know.

If we only could choose our relations
How happy, I'm certain, we'd be!
And just one thing more: I am perfectly sure
Mine all feel the same about me.

Fable

I was a slave on Samos, a small man
Carelessly put together; face a mask
So frightful that at first the people ran
Away from me, especially at dusk.

I was possessed, too, of a rattling tongue
That only now and then would let words pass
As they should properly be said or sung.
In general, you could say I was a mess.

One thing redeemed me. People marvelled at
The brilliance with which my speech was woven.
It was, they said, as if a toad had spat
Diamonds. And my ugliness was forgiven.

Soon I was freed, and sooner was the friend
Of kings and commoners who came a-calling.
Of my bright hoard of wit there seemed no end,
Nor of the tales that I rejoiced in telling.

But there were heads and hearts where, green and cold,
The seeds of envy and of hate were lying.
From our most sacred shrine, a cup of gold
Was hidden in my store, myself unknowing.

'Sacrilege! He is thief!' my accusers swore,
And to the cliffs of Delphi I was taken,
Hurled to the myrtle-scented valley floor
And on its whitest stones my body broken.

'This is the end of him and his poor fame!'
I heard them cry upon the gleaming air.
Stranger, now tell me if you know my name,
My story of the Tortoise and the Hare?

see Notes on p.102

45

Photograph

She walks among time-beaten stones
One hand upon the rood beam stair
That rises out of sticks and grass
Into a nothingness of air.

Here, where the abbey's great ship struck
And bramble bushes curve and sprout
She stands her granite-sprinkled ground
And stares the speering camera out.

She's dressed for Sunday: finest serge,
The high-necked blouse, a golden pin.
My grandmother: who sewed and scrubbed,
Cleaned out the church, took washing in.

Too soon, my mother said, too soon
The hands were white and washed to bone;
The seven children grown and gone,
And suddenly a life was done.

Today I stand where she once stood
And stranded arch and column sprawl,
Watching where still the ivy streams
In torrents down the abbey wall.

And still the many-noted rooks
About the tree-tops rail and run;
Still, at my feet, the celandine
Opens its gold star to the sun.

Firm as a figurehead she stands,
Sees with unsparing eye the thread
Of broken words within my hand
And will not turn away her head.

SEASON, LEGEND AND SPELL

In Canada

Walking down Beaver
I heard the stone river
Snap like a string.
Spring! you say. It is spring!

Walking down Buffalo
See where ice crystals, snow
Lift off brown grass.
Pass, summer, pass!

Walking down Wolf
Watch a single gold leaf
Sink and lie still.
Fall! you say. Fall!

Walking down Bear
I see afternoon air
Turn grey, turn blear.
Winter, you say, is here!

Walking down Beaver
Watch sky, tree uncover
Secret green, secret blue.
Still the great wheel turns true!

*The streets of the Canadian town of Banff,
in the Rocky Mountains, are named after
various native animals.*

50

Summer Was Always Sun

Summer was always sun,
Winter was made of snow,
Forward the spring, the fall
Was slow.

Down from the moor the
    stream
Ran swift, ran clear.
The trees were leaved with song
For all to hear.

The seas, the skies were blue.
With stars the beach was sown.
Printing the endless shore,
A child: barefoot, alone.

What is this time, this place?
I hear you say.
When was the wide world so?
Yesterday.

Bramblepark

Bramblepark Cottage
Bramblepark Well,
Sleep in the sound
Of St Stephen's bell.

Only the chimney-stack
Stands up high.
The cottage is burst
And roofed with sky.

The bright grass litters
Bramblepark Lane.
The wash-house tub
Is filled with rain.

Here's a rusted saw;
A broken crock.
A bath with no bottom
Brims nettle and dock.

The one-tree bridge
Is fallen and gone
Where the easy trout
Hid under a stone.

Here we blackberried,
Here we swam,
Made out of pebbles and mud
A dam.

Here the tall heron
Fished the stream.
Here we watched
The kingfisher gleam.

Down the long valley
The wood-pigeons cry
Where the Padstow to Waterloo
Train streamed by.

But when the day
Slides into the dark
Over the valley
At Bramblepark,

Whose is the voice
I know so well
Sounding within
The cottage shell?

And whose is the hand
That strikes a spark
For the evening lamp
At Bramblepark?

Is it the light
Of moon or star,
The little bold owl
Or the brown nightjar?

Do I hear or see?
Do I wake or dream?
Never you ask,
Says the changing stream.

Spell

When I was walking by Tamar stream
The day was sweet as honey and cream.
The air was brisk as a marriage bell.
(Kiss if you must, but never tell.)

When I was walking by Tamar flood
I plucked a rose the colour of blood.
The red ran out and the thorn ran in.
(Finish all, if you begin.)

When I was walking by
   Tamar brook
I met a man with a reaping hook.
The beard he wore was white as
   the may.
(The hours they run like water away.)

When I was walking by Tamar race
I met a maid with a smiling face.
Out of her eyes fell tears like rain.
(You will never see this road again.)

When I was walking by Tamar lock
I picked a bunch of sorrel and dock,
Creeping Jenny and hart's-tongue fern
(Days they go, but cannot return.)

When I was walking by Tamar spring
I found me a stone and a plain gold ring.
I stared at the sun, I stared at my shoes.
(Which do you choose? Which do you choose?)

The Twelve-o'clock Stone

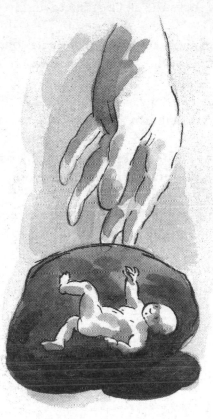

Lay the child of bending bone
At midnight on the granite stone.

When the bell tells twelve o'clock
Like a cradle it shall rock.

It shall swing and it shall sway
As if it sailed upon the bay.

Straight and strong his bones shall grow
As rocks the clock-stone to and fro;

Strong as the stone that he lies on,
Though he who rocks it, none has known.

There's not a wise man in the land
Knows that arm and knows that hand:

For he who rocks the midnight stone
Is not of man and woman born.

But when the bell tells twelve o'clock
Like a cradle it shall rock.

When lies a child as bare as bone
At midnight on the turning stone.

see Notes on p.103

Tavistock Goose Fair

The day my father took me to the Fair
Was just before he died of the First War.
We walked the damp, dry-leaved October air.
My father was twenty-seven and I was four.

The train was whistles and smoke and dirty steam.
I won myself a smudge of soot in the eye.
He tricked it out as we sat by a windy stream.
Farmers and gypsies were drunken-dancing by.

My dad wore his Irish cap, his riding-coat.
His boots and leggings shone as bright as a star.
He carried an ashling stick, stood soldier-straight.
The touch of his hand was strong as an iron bar.

The roundabout played 'Valencia' on the Square.
I heard the frightened geese in a wicker pen.
Out of his mouth an Indian man blew fire.
There was a smell of beer; cold taste of rain.

The cheapjacks bawled best crockery made of bone,
Solid silver spoons and cures for a cold.
My father bought a guinea for half-a-crown.
The guinea was a farthing painted gold.

Everyone else was tall. The sky went black.
My father stood me high on a drinking-trough.
I saw a man in chains escape from a sack.
I bothered in case a gypsy carried me off.

Today, I hardly remember my father's face;
Only the shine of his boot-and-legging leather
The day we walked the yellow October weather;
Only the way he strode at a soldier's pace
The way he stood like a soldier of the line;
Only the feel of his iron hand on mine.

*The Fair is still held every year at this Devonshire town
on the second Wednesday in October.*

On St Catherine's Day
(November 25th)

We are the Workhouse children,
Maids dressed in white,
Our gowns are trimmed with ribbon,
With flowers our hair is bright.

Before us walks the Master
With sure and steady tread,
And here is the tallest maid of all
A gilt crown on her head.

She bears in her hand a sceptre
Of yellow wood and tin,
And in the other a distaff
With which we may spin.

Pray give to us your ha'pennies
And give your farthings too,
That we may buy the wheels
    and reels
Our finest work to do.

On this day good St Catherine
To the sharp wheel has been,
Catherine, Saint of Spinners,
Catherine our Queen.

Today we shall eat rump steak
And we shall dance and game,
But the day is short and the year is long
Before it comes again.

We stand in church for the Parson,
We sit both straight and tall
As do the little stone children
That are beside the wall.

Our faces are white as paper,
Our hands are made of bone,
We may not speak the truth with our tongues
But with our eyes alone.

Though the Workhouse wall is broken,
With truest eye and clear
Watch for the Workhouse children,
For we are always here.

see Notes on p.103

The Apple-Tree Man

The farmer sleeps under a printed stone.
The farm it fell to the Youngest Son.
The Eldest has neither a hearth nor home.
   A sorrow and shame, said the Apple-Tree Man.

The Youngest he lends him an orchard green,
An ox and an ass and a handful of grain
And their Grannie's old cottage in Watery Lane.
   It's not what it sounds, said the Apple-Tree Man.

For the grain it was mouldy, the roof it had flown,
And never a fruit had the apple-trees grown,
The dunk was all skin and the ox was all bone.
   Here's a how-do-ye-do, said the Apple-Tree Man.

The Eldest he neither did mutter nor moan.
He found all the slates and he nailed them back on.
He laid the grass low that was lanky and long.
   Will-o'-the-Work! said the Apple-Tree Man.

He cured him his beasts with the words of a charm.
The ox and the ass to the orchard are gone,
And the apple-trees flourish as never they've done.
   Sun's coming up, said the Apple-Tree Man.

Said Youngest to Eldest, 'Now pray understand
When Quarter Day comes you must pay on demand
And dap down the rent on the palm of my hand.'
    Brotherly love! said the Apple-Tree Man.

But the Eldest had hardly the price of a pin.
Though he worked and he worried his profit was thin.
'It's wrecked and it's ruined,' he said, 'that I am!'
    Can't have that, said the Apple-Tree Man.

Two days before Christmas, all catch as catch can,
The Youngest he gives the old orchard a scan.
'Did you never hear tell of the treasure within?'
    Brother's heard of it now, said the Apple-Tree Man.

'Day after tomorrow when midnight is come
And the beasts in the shippen no longer are dumb
To task 'em and ask 'em,' he said, 'is my plan.'
    They'll tell you no lies, said the Apple-Tree Man.

'So brother,' the Youngest said, 'wake me betimes
Before Christmas comes and the church clock it chimes
And a sixpence I'll slice off your rent for a span.'
    Such bounteousness! said the Apple-Tree Man.

But the Eldest hangs holly all up in a chain
And he gives to the ox the sweet hay and good grain
And to the old donkey he gives just the same.
    Wassail! Wassail! said the Apple-Tree Man.

Then the Eldest his cider mug fills to the brim
And gives to his apple-trees out in the dim.
'I wish you Good Christmas,' he says, 'where you stand!'
   Look under my roots, said the Apple-Tree Man.

Says the Eldest, 'I'm blest, but it's magic that's planned
For the earth and the stones are all softer than sand.'
And a chest full of gold he digs up with his hands.
   Bide quiet and hide it, says the Apple-Tree Man.

At midnight the Eldest calls Youngest to rise
And down he comes running, the sleep in his eyes.
'Dear ox and dear donkey, please tell if you can
Where lies the gold treasure that's under my land?'

The gold and the treasure are taken and gone
And you never shall find it by moon or by sun
Though all the wide world you may search and may scan,
  Said the ox and the ass and the Apple-Tree Man.

The source of this story is a legend from Somerset
documented in Folk Tales of England *edited by*
Katharine M. Briggs and Ruth L. Tongue (Routledge,
1965) and also Katharine Briggs' A Dictionary of
Fairies *(Allen Lane, 1976). The Apple-Tree Man was*
the name given to the oldest apple-tree in an orchard,
and in which the fertility of the entire orchard was
thought to dwell.
  According to an ancient custom in this part of
Britain, it was the youngest and not the eldest son who
inherited a property on the death of the parent. By
virtue of his age, the eldest son was assumed to have
had time to make his way, and make good in the world.
In the story here, the eldest was regarded with favour
by the Apple-Tree Man because he saw to the restora-
tion of the health and fertility of the ruined orchard,
and also because he wassailed the trees by pouring
draughts of cider over them: a custom still followed in
certain districts of Somerset.

JACK AND COMPANY

Jack the Treacle Eater

Here comes Jack the Treacle Eater,
Never swifter, never sweeter,
With a peck of messages,
Some long, some shorter,
From my Lord and Master's quarter
(Built like a minaret)
Somewhere in Somerset.
   Jack, how do you make such speed
   From banks of Tone to banks of Tweed
   And all the way back?
   'I train on treacle,' says Jack.

Here's one for Sam Snoddy
(Cantankerous old body).
'Will you come for Christmas dinner
With Missus and Squire?'
'Not on your life,' says Sam.
'Rather eat bread and jam
By my own fire.'
   Jack, how do you trot so spry
   The long road to Rye
   Bearing that heavy pack?
   'I train on treacle,' says Jack.

Here's one for Sally Bent
Lives in a gypsy tent
Down at Land's End.
'Will you sing at my daughter's bridal?'
'No,' says Sally. 'I'm too idle.
Besides, I've not much choice
Since up to Bodmin I lost my voice.'
 Jack, how do you travel so light
 From morning star through half the night
 With never a snack?
 'I train on treacle,' says Jack.

Here's one for Trooper Slaughter,
Retired, of Petherwin Water.
'Dear Tom, will you come
And we'll talk of our days with the drum,
Bugle, fife and the cannon's thunder.'
'Too late,' says Tom, 'old chum.
I'm already six feet under.'
 Jack, how do you care for your wife
 If you run all the days of your life?
 Is it something the rest of us lack?
 'I train on treacle,' says Jack.

The original Jack lived in Somerset and was a famous
runner who took messages to and from London for
the Messiter family of Barwick Park, near Yeovil.
He is said to have trained on treacle, and is
commemorated there by one of four follies (useless
but usually delightful and expensive buildings put
up for fun) built by George Messiter in the early
nineteenth century. On top of Jack's Folly is a figure
of Hermes (representing Jack), the Greek messenger
and herald of the gods. At midnight, Jack is said to
climb down from his Folly and go to the lake by the
great house in order to quench his tremendous thirst
caused by eating so much treacle.

There Was a Young Snowman

There was a young snowman of Churton-le-Grice*
Who made up his mind he would stay in one piece,
And whether the weather was hot or was cool
He'd never turn into a puddle or pool.

Each winter-white night when the
   temperature fell
He took off his scarf and his topper
   as well,
He took off his jacket, and all on
   his own
He froze himself solid as iron or stone.

In springtime the swallows around
   him all flew.
In summer he smiled in the green and
   the blue.
In autumn he watched the leaves skim
   down the lane,
And in winter he froze up all over again.

But soon the good people of Churton-le-Grice
Grew weary of hearing (and quite without cease),
'It's a cold-hearted folk who live here, I'll be bound,
Where even a snowman lasts all the year round!'

So the Churtoners built them a battering ram.
They lit a big bonfire. They all shouted, 'Scram!'
They pushed with a tractor, they pulled with a trawl,
But they just couldn't shift the young snowman at all.

'It's simple,' they said, 'and quite perfectly plain
That this singular snowman would rather remain.
We must pay no regard to what others may say.
If he likes us *that* much, why not ask him to stay?'

And if on your travels, for any good reason,
You happen by Churton (whatever the season)
Remember the snowman who stood on the hill
In yesterday's weather. You'll find him there still.

*pronounced 'Greece'

The Song of the Shapes

Miss Triangle, Miss Rectangle,
   Miss Circle and Miss Square
Went walking down on Shipshape Shore
   To taste the sea-salt air.
They talked of this, they talked of that,
   From a, b, c, to z.
But most of all they talked about
   The day they would be wed.

'My sweetheart is a sailor blue!'
   Miss Circle sang with joy,
'And dreams of me when out at sea
   Or swinging round the buoy;
When homeward bound for Plymouth Sound
   Or sailing by the Nore,
Or gazing through the port-hole
   At some shining foreign shore.

'And when we both are married,
   Up at the Villa Sphere
We'll have a Christmas pudding
   Each evening of the year;
And ring-a-ring o'-roses
   We'll dance at night and noon,
Whether the sun is shining
   Or if it is the moon.'

'Good gracious!' cried Miss Triangle,
   'But it's quite plain to see
What might be best for you
      and yours
   Won't do for mine and me.
He plays the balalaika
   In a Russian Gypsy Band
All up and down the country
   And in many a foreign land.

'He loves the dusty desert,
   The camels and the sun,
And sits and thinks beside the Sphinx
Of when we shall be one.
He's bought for us a dream-house
   By shady palm-trees hid.
Do say you all will pay a call
   At Little Pyramid.'

'My boy so rare,' then said Miss Square,
  'Is different yet again.
His world is one of timber,
  Of chisel and of plane.
I might have wed a constable,
  I might have wed a vet,
But fairly on a carpenter
  My heart is squarely set.

'Our own dear home won't be a cone,
  A cylinder (or tube),
But just a quiet cottage
  At the village of All Cube.
And you must come and visit us
  Each Saturday at three
For sticky buns and cake (with plums)
  And sugar-lumps and tea.'

'Though pleasant,' sighed Miss Rectangle,
  'To walk among these rocks is,
I'd sooner far be where my dar-
  ling's making cardboard boxes.
He makes them big, he makes them small,
  He makes them short and long,
And all the day (his workmates say)
  He sings a sort of song.

'My bride and I one day will fly
  Beside the Spanish sea
And live in Casa Cuboid
  Which we've built above the quay.
It has a special corner
  For fishing with a line
And catching of fish-fingers
  For friends who come to dine.'

Miss Triangle, Miss Rectangle,
  Miss Circle and Miss Square
Came walking up from Shipshape Shore
  Without a single care.
But pray remember if you play
  The match and marriage game
Opposites often suit as well
  As those who seem the same.

Willoughby

Willoughby Whitebody-Barrington-Trew
Could never decide what the weather would do.
Out of his window he'd gaze by the hour
To see if it might be a shine or a shower.
He'd open the closet that's under the stair
And he'd hem and he'd haw as to what he should wear,
And often as not (and I'm stating a fact)
By the time he set off it was time to come back.

He'd wait by the hat-stand inside the front door
And ask himself hundreds of questions, or more.
'Will it snow? Will it blow? Will it rain? Will it hail?
Will these summery breezes turn into a gale?
Is the temperature likely to rise or to fall?
Do you think that we're in for a bit of a squall?
Although the sun's shining,' he'd say with a groan,
'It'll come down in buckets before I get home.'

'Shall I get me a waterproof? Put on a coat?
An ulster that buttons right up to my throat?
A bowler? A beret? A felt or a straw?
The finest glengarry that ever you saw?
Am I needing a panama hat or a cane?
A carriage-umbrella to keep off the rain?
Is it Wellington weather or sandal or shoe?
I'm ashamed to confess that I haven't a clue.
There's no doubt about it,' said Willoughby White,
'Whatever I do I just can't get it right –
And if folk say I'm crazy I don't care a jot,
So I might as well go out dressed up in the lot.'

And every item in closet and hall
He took until nothing was left there at all.
'You may sneer,' declared Willoughby, 'or you may scoff,
But if it's too hot you can take something off.'
And he'd say to himself till his breath was all gone,
'If you haven't it with you, you can't put it on.'
Said Willoughby Whitebody-Barrington who
Could never decide what the weather would do.

Give Me a House

Give me a house, said Polly.
Give me land, said Hugh.
Give me the moon, said Sadie.
Give me the sun, said Sue.

Give me a horse, said Rollo.
Give me a hound, said Joe.
Give me fine linen, said Sarah.
Give me silk, said Flo.

Give me a mountain, said Kirsty.
Give me a valley, said Jim.
Give me a river, said Dodo.
Give me the sky, said Tim.

Give me the ocean, said Adam.
Give me a ship, said Hal.
Give me a kingdom, said Rory.
Give me a crown, said Sal.

Give me gold, said Peter.
Give me silver, said Paul.
Give me love, said Jenny,
Or nothing at all.

SEA AND SHORE

Morwenstow

Where do you come from, sea,
To the sharp Cornish shore,
Leaping up to the raven's crag?
  From Labrador.

Do you grow tired, sea?
Are you weary ever
When the storms burst over your head?
  Never.

Are you hard as a diamond, sea,
As iron, as oak?
Are you stronger than flint or steel?
  And the lightning stroke.

Ten thousand years and more, sea,
You have gobbled your fill,
Swallowing stone and slate!
   I am hungry still.

When will you rest, sea?
   When moon and sun
   Ride only fields of salt water
   And the land is gone.

Dan Dory

Today I saw Dan Dory
Walking out of the sea.
'Did you tell the world my story?'
Dan said to me.

Salt glittered on his breast, his fingers.
Drops of gold fell from his hair.
The look in his eye was sapphire-bright
As he stood there.

'Your head is white,' said Dan Dory.
'Trenched your face, your hand.
And why do you walk to greet me
So slowly across the sand?'

'I watched you held, Dan Dory,
In ocean fast.
Thirty, no, forty years ago
I saw you last.

'And I now see you older
By not a second's stroke
Than when the sun raged overhead
And the sea was flame, was smoke.'

'Did you tell the world my story?'
I heard him say.
'And for the unwisdom of the old
Do the young still pay?'

'Still spins the water and the land,'
I said, 'as yesterday' –
And leaned to take his hand. But he
Had vanished away.

Serena

Serena lies under the waterfall
In the blue sound of the sea.
Soft and sweet I hear her sing
By the feathery tamarisk tree,
Its flowers pink, its flowers white,
She sings all through the moonwashed night.
Who do you sing for, Serena?
   Teach your song to me.

Do you sing for the healthy farmer
Or the sailor on the quay?
Is it for Tom the Drover
Or the lawyer with his fee?
Do you sing for the pedlar with his pack,
Or Schoolie, or Silly Strong-Arm Jack?
Who do you sing for, Serena?
   Teach your song to me.

Do you sing your song for a beggar
Or the banker with fortunes three?
Is it he who swims the valley stream
Or the climber on the scree?
Is your song for the soldier on the square,
The boy on the hunter, the boy in the air?
'For none of you,' says Serena.
    'Nor shall it ever be.'

Francesco de la Vega

Francesco de la Vega
From the hours of childhood
Passed his days
In the salt of the ocean.

Only one word he spoke.
Lierjanes! – the name
Of the sea-village of his birth
In the Year of God 1657.

While other children
Helped in field or kitchen,
Wandered the mountain-slope,
He swam the wild bay.

While others were at church
He dived to where lobster and squid
Lodged in the sea's dark cellar.
He must suffer a salt death,
   said Father Ramiro.

His mother and father entreated him
To come to his own bed.
His brothers and sisters called him
Home from the yellow sand-bar.

Amazed, they watched him
Arrow the waves like a young dolphin.
Until they tired of waiting, he hid
Under the mountain of black water.

On a night mad with storm
The waves rose high as the church-tower
And beat the shore like a drum.
He did not return with the morning.

Foolish boy, now he is drowned, they said.
His family added their salt tears to the ocean
As they cast on flowers and prayers.
In my opinion, he asked for it,
  said Father Ramiro.

Years flowed by: ten, twenty.
The village of Lierjanes forgot him.
Then, miles off Cadiz, herring fishermen
Sighted, at dawning, a sea-creature.

Three days they pursued him
Through the autumn waters;
Trapped him at last in strong nets
And brought him to land.

They gazed at his silver body in wonder;
At his pale eyes, staring always ahead;
At his hair, tight, and as a red moss.
What seemed like bright scales adorned his spine.

Most marvellous of all, instead
Of nails upon his feet and hands
There grew strange shells
That glowed gently like jewels of the sea.

When they questioned him
All he would reply was, *Lierjanes!*
Wrapping him in a soft white sailcloth
They laid him on a bed of linen.

A monk of Cadiz heard their story.
It is Francesco de la Vega,
The fish-boy of Lierjanes, he declared.
I shall bring him to his home and family.

Ah, but how his parents, brothers, sisters
Wept with happiness and welcomed him
With loving kisses and embraces, as though
Like Lazarus he had risen, and from a sea-grave!

But the young man returned no sign
Of love or recognition.
He gazed at them as though sightless;
Was indifferent to their sighs, their fondlings.

Long years he dwelt among them,
Never speaking, eating little,
Shifting unhappily in the decent clothes
With which they arrayed him.

One morning, nine years on,
He vanished from the house and hearth-side;
Was seen no more in the village of Lierjanes.
Great was the sadness of those who loved him!

Months, years ahead, two fishermen
Hauling across the stubborn waters
Of the Bay of Asturias
Sighted a sudden sea-creature at play.

Swiftly, and with a spear and net,
They followed, but he escaped them.
As he rushed through the waves they heard a cry.
Lierjanes! Lierjanes!

The Parson and the Clerk

The Clerk stands in the ocean,
The Parson on the land,
From top to toe to fingertips
Red as the Devon sand.

The people of Teignmouth say
(And they say it at Shaldon, too)
That the Parson and the Clerk
Are standstone through and through,

And the story of how they came home
Rather more drunk than dry
From a night with the Bishop of Exeter
Is nothing more than a lie.

And there never was a storm
As they drove beside the bay
That washed the horses to Babbicombe
And the Parson and Clerk away.

Though when the morning came
Along the salted shore
There stood two pillars of stone
That never stood there before.

And often, some folk say,
If you stand quite still and hark,
The Parson is taking a service
With responses from the Clerk.

But only the Parson and Clerk
Know the truth of the tale
And gently both of them wink an eye
As they stand on the sand and shale.

Says the Parson to the Clerk,
'Perhaps it is just as well
For the sake of their peace of mind
That they think we are stone and shell.

'And whether the day is bright
Or the night is wild and dark
Shall we let them believe it so?'
'Amen,' says the Clerk.

This is a legend of Devonshire. If you have travelled
by train along the coast-line between Dawlish and
Teignmouth, beyond Exeter, you will have passed the
two rocks known as the Parson and the Clerk. 'Clerk'
was the name given to a specially appointed layman
whose duties included helping the parson at baptisms
and marriages, and who also led the responses made
by the church congregation during prayers.

Teignmouth

Teignmouth. Ox-red
Sand and scree.
The pier's long finger
Testing the sea.

Salt-damp deck-chairs
Along the Den.
Pierrots singing,
Here we are again!

Sand-artist crimping
The crocodile:
Quartz for a yellow eye,
Shells for a smile.

Punch kills the Baby.
The Mission sings a hymn.
Through the level water
The sailboats swim.

My father, slick
From his boots to his cap,
Driving the Doctor's
Pony and trap.

Here's my mother,
Lives next door,
Strolling with a sun-shade
The long blue shore.

The sun and the day
Burn gold, burn green.
August Bank Holiday,
1914.

In with the evening
The tide turns grey;
Washes a world
Away, away.

NOTES

Rocco

The fourteenth-century St Roche, born in Montpellier, was the patron saint of those suffering from the plague. He spent a great part of his life on pilgrimages. While ministering to the sick in Italy, he himself caught the plague in the town of Piacenza. Desperately ill, he retired to the woods to die. A story tells that here he was discovered by a dog who licked his wounds and each day brought him a fresh loaf of bread. In early paintings, St Roche is usually shown wearing a cockleshell (the badge of the pilgrim) in his hat, and is accompanied by his faithful dog. In the church of St Thomas-the Apostle (where I was christened) at Launceston in Cornwall is a faded medieval wall-painting of St Roche and his dog.

Rock Ape

The huge rocks called the Pillars of Hercules guard the western entrance to the Mediterranean (or Middle) Sea. One is Gibraltar; on the other stands the town of Ceuta in North Africa. Gibraltar (Gebal-al-Tarik, the Hill of Tarik) takes its name from Tarik, the Moorish leader who fortified it in AD 711. It is a part of the world rich in myth and fable. One legend tells of how the famous Barbary apes who live on Gibraltar originally came to the Rock from Africa by means of a secret tunnel under the sea.

Fable

Perhaps it's appropriate that the most famous writer of fables, known to us as Aesop, also has what are probably a great many unhistorical and legendary stories told about his life. The poem collects some of these 'facts' together: including the belief that he had a stammer. If Aesop was one person (and not, as some scholars say, merely the name given to a whole group of story-tellers) it is at least fairly certain that he lived in about the sixth century BC.

The Twelve-o'clock Stone

In Cornwall are a number of logan-stones: great poised boulders capable of rocking to and fro at a gentle touch. At Nancledra, in West Penwith, is such a stone: but with a difference. It was believed impossible to move it by human hand at any time, though precisely at midnight it was said to rock of its own accord like a cradle. In early times, children suffering from rickets (a disease causing a softening of the bones and resulting in such ailments as curvature of the spine and bow-legs) were brought and laid on the stone in the hope of a cure.

On St Catherine's Day

In Victorian times, girls living in the local workhouse were led in procession round the town by the workhouse Master. They stopped and sang before the houses of important local people, and were later given money, a special dinner and tea, and were allowed to play games in the evening. This all took place on the Feast Day of the martyred St Catherine of Alexandria who in the fourth century had been tortured on a spiked wheel (the Catherine wheel). St Catherine is the patron saint of young girls, and also of all whose work is connected with the wheel, such as spinners, millers and wheelwrights. Females in the old workhouses were employed on spinning.

Index of First Lines